HOW ?

HISTORY OPENS WINDOWS

T

Printed in China

Produced by Celia Floyd

04
10

Library of Congress Cataloging-in-Publication Data

Shuter, Jane.
    The ancient Romans / Jane Shuter.
    p.   cm. -- (History opens windows)
    Includes bibliographical references and index.
    Summary: An introduction to the various elements of ancient Roman
civilization, including gods and goddesses, clothing, food, town and
country life, government, and the army.
    ISBN 1-57572-591-6 (lib. bdg.). --ISBN 1-57572-592-4 (pbk.)
    1. Rome--Civilization--Juvenile literature.   [1. Rome--
Civilization.].   I. Title. II. Series.
DG78.S48   1997
937--dc21   97-15072
                                                                  CIP
                                                                  AC

Acknowledgments

The author and publishers are grateful to the following for permission to
reproduce copyright photographs:

British Museum, p. 6, 16, 20 (left); C. M. Dixon, p. 8, 18;
Veralanium Museum, p. 10; Ancient Art & Architecture Collection Ltd./Ronald
Sheridan, p. 12, 22, 25; Bridgeman Art Library/Giraudon, p. 14; British Library,
p. 20 (right); Scala Photo Library, Italy, p. 24; Hamlyn Group Picture Library,
p. 26; Rheinischen Landesmuseums, Trier, Germany, p. 28.

Cover photograph © Gilles Mermet, Giraudon

Every effort has been made to contact copyright holders of any material
reproduced in this book. Any omissions will be rectified in subsequent printings
if notice is given to the publisher.

Some words are shown in bold, **like this**. You can find out what they mean
by looking in the glossary.

Contents

Introduction

The Roman Empire grew outwards from Rome, Italy. This map shows the empire at its biggest, in about A.D.100.

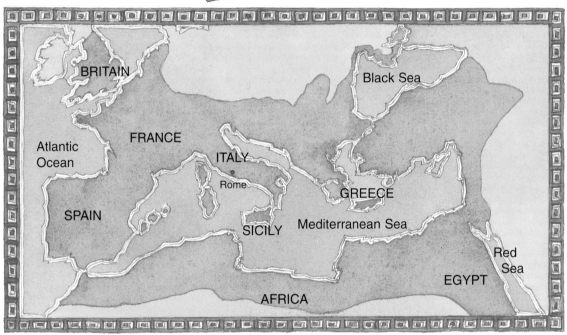

BRITAIN

Black Sea

Atlantic Ocean

FRANCE

ITALY

Rome

SPAIN

GREECE

Mediterranean Sea

SICILY

Red Sea

EGYPT

AFRICA

576 B.C. Rome becomes a city

241 B.C. Sicily the first Roman province

Kings ruled Rome

Roman Republic

800 B.C.

500 B.C.

100 B.C.

The Romans captured and ruled many places between about 500 B.C. and A.D. 476. The center of their huge **empire** was Rome, Italy.

By about 265 B.C., Rome controlled most of Italy. It kept growing. Sometimes the Roman army captured a country. As Rome grew stronger, some countries did not want to fight. They were happy to become part of Rome. They wanted the Roman army to protect them. Each new country became a **province** of Rome, run by a Roman governor. In return for Roman protection, the provinces paid **taxes** to Rome and obeyed Roman laws.

The Roman Empire kept spreading until it got too big and it could not keep everyone safe. Slowly, it lost its provinces and its power.

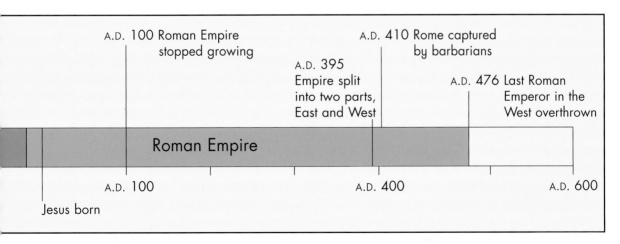

A.D. 100 Roman Empire stopped growing

A.D. 395 Empire split into two parts, East and West

A.D. 410 Rome captured by barbarians

A.D. 476 Last Roman Emperor in the West overthrown

Roman Empire

A.D. 100   A.D. 400   A.D. 600

Jesus born

How Rome was Ruled

At first, kings ruled Rome when it was a small part of Italy. This period lasted about 200 years. But in 509 B.C., the Romans threw out their king. They made Rome into a **republic**.

The Roman Republic was governed by wealthy and important Roman men called **patricians**. These men were part of the **Senate**. The Senate gave advice to two ruling **consuls**, who changed each year. All men, patricians and **plebeians**, chose the consuls. Plebeians were supposed to have a say in how things were run. Some of the time they had more say than other times.

When they took over another country, the Romans made new coins to celebrate. These coins celebrate the capture of Egypt and Armenia.

The Roman Republic grew. The Senate took more and more power and land. The difference between wealthy and poor people grew. Patricians, plebeians, governors of **provinces**, and members of the army all scrambled for power. It was hard to govern when these people did not work together.

The Romans needed a strong leader to unite everyone. Julius Caesar was an army general who tried to unite the republic. However, he was murdered in 44 B.C. Finally, the strongest of the consuls, Augustus, took over the powers of the Senate. He was the first emperor, a kind of king.

*A big **empire** needed a lot of record-keeping. These officials wrote information down on paper scrolls and wax tablets. You can see the scrolls and tablets stacked on the shelves.*

The Army

The Roman army was an important reason why the **empire** grew so large. At first, every Roman man had to fight. Wealthy men fought on horseback, common men fought on foot.

As the empire grew, fighting became a full-time, paid job. Roman soldiers were well-trained, well-organized, and well-equipped. Men from all over the empire joined the army. A soldier joined the army for 15 to 20 years. At the end of this time, he was given land to farm or money to buy land.

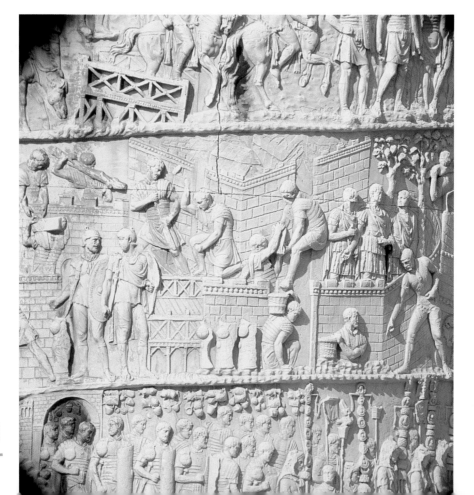

Roman soldiers had to build things as well as fight. They had to make forts and roads and bridges to cross rivers.

*A common Roman soldier
and his equipment.*

*A Roman soldier's
gear weighed
about 77 pounds.*

*Body armor
was made up
of separate
pieces, not
one stiff
piece. This
made it easier
for the soldier
to move.*

*Soldiers
held shields
over their
heads when
attacking
a wall.*

*Each soldier
carried two
poles. They were
used to build a
fence when the
army made
a camp.*

*Nails were placed on the bottom
of soldiers' sandals. This helped
them get a good grip on muddy
ground.*

9

Builders and Engineers

The Romans needed good roads. The army had to move quickly. Orders from Rome had to be taken to all the **provinces**. So Roman **engineers** built a network of roads all across the **empire**.

Engineers used their skills to design huge buildings and long bridges. They also designed **aqueducts** to carry clean water to towns and cities. Many of these things were so well built that they are still standing today.

The Pont du Gard aqueduct today. It carried water to the Roman town of Nîmes. The arches give strong support to the channel that carried the water.

Building a Road

The first step was to decide where
the road should go. Engineers
measured from one high point
to another, making the roads
as straight as they could.

The builders then dug a trench. The
road was built up in the trench in
layers. First there was a layer of
big stones. Next came a layer of
gravel. This leveled off any bumps
made by the big stones. Then
came a layer of sand and cement.

The top layer was big, flat stones
fitted tightly together and packed
down hard. Roads were slightly
higher in the middle than at the
sides so water could drain off.

Gods and Goddesses

The Romans believed in many gods and goddesses, who could come to earth and change anyone's life. So it was important to keep the gods happy. The Romans built large **temples** to their gods, like Jupiter, who were worshipped throughout the **empire**. Smaller temples were built to less important gods. When Romans became Christians, they had to give up all their other gods.

Most people had a shrine in their homes. They prayed to the lares, or household gods, at this shrine. They also prayed to their dead relatives.

A small temple to the goddess Minerva. Temples were built in this style all over the empire.

If a new province had different gods, the Romans accepted them. When the Romans conquered Greece, they found that the Greek gods were like their own. For example, the Greek god Zeus was like the Roman god Jupiter, and the Greek goddess Hera was like the Roman goddess Juno.

13

Town Life

Roman towns and cities were busy places. The biggest and most important city in the empire was Rome. But many smaller towns all over the empire had all the things the people needed.

A Roman town needed a forum. This was a large central square with shops and temples. People met here to do business or talk politics. A town needed at least one public bath house, a theater, and many houses, shops, and workshops.

A butcher's shop. The butcher is cutting meat. Cut pieces hang from hooks and there is a bowl to throw the bones and fat into.

14

A small Roman town. People came to it from all around to buy and sell things in the market.

Country Life

Most Romans lived and worked in the countryside. They grew crops to feed the **empire**. People in different parts of the empire grew different crops, depending on the soil and the weather. In hot parts they grew grapes and olives. In cold parts they grew turnips and apples. Most farmers grew wheat for flour.

Some people worked for themselves on small farms. They grew enough food to feed their families, with maybe a little left over to sell at the local market. Other people worked on large farms on lands that belonged to rich **patricians**.

This statue of a farmer plowing with oxen was found in Britain. Oxen were used on farms all over the empire.

A patrician's villa. The villa was the main house on an estate. It was a country house for the patrician, but it was also the main farm. Very wealthy families had several villas, much grander than this one.

These are the barns for storing food and for housing animals.

Workers grew small amounts of vegetables in the yard, such as peppers and lettuce, as well as growing crops in the fields.

Family Life

The Romans had very clear ideas about how families should be run. The paterfamilias, or father, was the head of the family. Everyone had to obey him, even his grown-up children. Men were supposed to work and do business outside the home. Women were supposed to run the home and look after children.

All but the poorest families had **slaves** to work for them. Slaves were part of the family. They were mostly people who had been captured in battle. Some were well treated, others were not. Slaves could buy their freedom if they could save enough money.

A carving from Rome of a mother bathing her baby with the help of a slave.

A wealthy family's home.

Slaves tidy the bedroom, while the son's wife dresses. Her baby is asleep in the cradle.

The daughter and her friends have a late breakfast. Her mother gives orders to the cook.

The father and his son are in the study.

Slaves keep the fire going for the hypocaust, or heating system.

The floor is raised on pillars. Warm air goes under the floor and rises to heat the house.

A slave takes a visitor to see the father.

Children

Children started school at the age of seven. Most boys went to school. Girls of wealthy families went to school and learned to run a home. Girls of poor families learned to spin, weave, cook, and clean. At school, children learned to read and write Latin and Greek and do math. Boys spent more time at school than girls.

When they were 15 years old, boys were considered adults. They finished school and could work, marry, and vote. Girls could marry after they were 14 years old. However, not many people married this young. Even if a boy married, he had to obey his father until the father died. A girl had to obey the head of the family she married into.

On the left is a doll with pieces from a race game. The pieces at top-right are knuckle bones used to play catch.

Roman children were looked after by their mothers until they were about seven years old.

After this, boys spent most of their time with their teachers and friends.

Girls saw more of their mothers, since women were supposed to stay at home together.

Food

The Romans ate three meals a day. Breakfast was bread with honey or fruit. Lunch was bread, olives, and cheese, or food left over from the day before.

For the main meal, everyone ate bread, fruit, and vegetables. They drank wine and sweetened other foods and drinks with honey. Unlike wealthy people, poor people did not eat meat every day. Rich people ate huge main meals, especially on special occasions. Giraffes, larks, and dormice were often served, not for the flavor, but because they cost a lot.

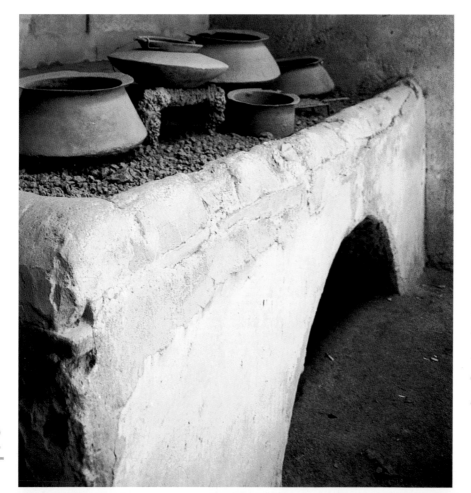

Romans cooked on iron stands over a fire. The fire was made on the top of a stone cooking table like this. Bread and roast meats were cooked in brick ovens.

A wealthy family's kitchen

People ate mostly chicken and pork. They also hunted meat, like this wild hare.

This slave is grinding spices. Expensive spices came from all over the empire.

Most people drank wine.

Romans ate lying down, propped up on their elbows. The food was served on low tables.

Entertainment

Most Romans went into towns for entertainment. They went to the theater to watch plays, listen to music, and see dancers and acrobats.

Some towns had an **arena**, which could be used for **chariot** racing. People would bet on who would win. Races were dangerous. Chariot drivers were often killed or injured.

Even more violent were the Games. Wild animals were let lose in the arena to fight each other. Sometimes criminals were put into the area to fight animals. Often they did not have weapons, or they were tied up. There was no way they could win.

A mosaic showing gladiators fighting each other in the arena.

Gladiators, or trained fighters, fought each other. Fights were often to the death. Gladiators were criminals or slaves. Some of them fought hard and lived long enough to buy their freedom. Most died fighting.

Romans also enjoyed less violent sports. They could go to the baths, where there were places to exercise. They could race, wrestle, or play handball. Then, when they were tired, they could use the baths and go home for dinner at about 4:00 p.m.

The Colosseum in Rome was the biggest Roman arena. Games held there went on for days. They even flooded the arena for sea battles!

25

Baths

The Romans thought it was very important to keep clean. Almost every town had public baths that anyone could use. Men and women went to separate public baths.

Wealthy people also had bath areas in their homes. These bath areas had hot, warm, and cold pools, too. This does not mean that wealthy people never went to the public baths. Romans went to the baths for more than just bathing. It was a social occasion, too. There were cool, warm, and hot pools of water to swim in. There were steam rooms and places to exercise. **Slaves** worked at the baths, massaging people and oiling and cleaning them.

People took an oil flask and strigil, or scraper, like these, to the baths. Romans did not use soap. Instead, a slave oiled the person all over. Then they scraped off the oil. Dirt and dead skin came off, too.

The cold bath. People often exercised in a special area outside the baths before going to the cold room.

The hot room was hot and steamy. The water was hot, too. There was a bowl of cold water to splash in to cool down.

The next room was the warm room. In a big bath house it would have a warm pool.

People left their clothes on shelves in the changing room.

A hypocaust heated the rooms. The furnace heated the air for the hypocaust and the water.

27

Clothes

Most people, except the poor, wore linen underwear, usually a loose tunic. What they wore over this depended on who they were.

Men wore an outer tunic that came to about the knees. This was usually made of wool. All men except **slaves** could wear a toga, a kind of cloak folded over one shoulder and draped around the body. Women wore a long tunic that reached to the ankles. They usually wore a long cloak to go out. Children wore similar clothes to adults.

This model of a plowman was made in Germany. People who worked outdoors in the colder provinces wore a thick, warm wool cape with a hood. It was oiled to keep out the wind and the rain.

Most clothes were made from cloth that was white, cream, or one color. Sometimes tunics had a single colored stripe around the edges or that ran from top to bottom. Clothes were usually washed in laundries, especially in towns.

This man wore clothes made of thick wool in winter. In summer he wore thin wool. His boots were leather.

In winter, this woman also wore clothes made of wool. In summer, she would wear thin wool or expensive silk.

Children and slaves dressed more simply than adults. They had simpler hairstyles, too.

End of the Empire

The Roman **Empire** got too big and too difficult to govern. By A.D. 100 it had stopped growing. In A.D. 395, the empire was split into two parts, east and west. This made it easier to govern. But **barbarians** began to raid **provinces** on the edges of the empire. The army could not defend every province. So the Romans left some places. In A.D. 410, barbarians captured Rome. In A.D. 476 only the Eastern Empire was left. The old Roman Empire had collapsed.

Barbarians attack a town in Roman Britain. Places like Britain, which were on the edges of the empire, were taken over first.

Glossary

aqueduct   This is a bridge that carries water from one place to another.

arena   This is a flat, open place in the middle of a circular theater.

barbarians   These were people from outside the Roman Empire.

chariot   This is a small, horse-drawn vehicle.

consuls   These were the two people who ran the Roman Republic.

empire   This is a group of territories or lands controlled by one country.

engineer   This is a person who designs and builds bridges and roads.

patricians   These were wealthy, important Roman men.

plebeians   These were common Roman men.

provinces   These were areas outside Italy controlled by Rome.

republic   This is a way of running the country, using people chosen by some citizens of that country.

Senate   This was the group of wealthy and important men who ran the Roman Republic.

slave   This is a person who belongs to someone else and can be bought and sold.

taxes   This is money you have to pay the government that runs the country.

temple   This is a place where people worship their gods or god.

More Books to Read

Brandt, Keith. *Ancient Rome*. Mahwah, N. J.: Troll Communications, 1985.

Cortes, Jose. *The Roman Empire*. Danbury, Conn: Childrens Press, 1993.

Guittard, Charles. *The Romans: Life in the Empire*. Brookfield, Conn: Millbrook Press, 1992.

Index